KU-518-711

— 55 COUNTRY — DOUGHCRAFT DESIGNS

LINDA ROGERS

David & Charles

This book is dedicated to the memory of my
grandmother, Bertha Amelia Johnson, business-
woman and craftsperson, in whose footsteps I'd like
to think I could follow.

Page 2 Duck wall plaque (see page 111)

The designs featured in this book are available commercially
as finished items. Further information is available from
'Dough Designs', The Old School, Gretton Road,
Gotherington, Cheltenham, Gloucestershire GL52 4EP. It is
an infringement of the law of copyright to copy these designs
for commercial purposes.

A DAVID & CHARLES BOOK

Photography by Paul Biddle
Illustrations by Lorraine Harrison

Copyright Text and Designs © Linda Rogers 1994, 1996
Copyright Photographs © David & Charles 1994, 1996
First published 1994
Reprinted 1994, 1995, 1996
First paperback edition 1996

Linda Rogers has asserted her right to be identified
as author of this work in accordance with the Copyright,
Designs and Patents Act 1988.

All rights reserved. No part of this publication may be
reproduced, stored in a retrieval system, or transmitted, in any
form or by any means, electronic or mechanical, by photocopying,
recording or otherwise, without prior permission in writing from
the publisher.

A catalogue record for this book is available
from the British Library.

ISBN 0 7153 0168 3 hardback
ISBN 0 7153 0606 5 paperback

Typeset by Ace Filmsetting Ltd, Frome
and printed in Great Britain by Butler & Tanner Ltd
for David & Charles
Brunel House Newton Abbot Devon

CONTENTS

INTRODUCTION

A wonderful piece of old German folklore tells that a piece of *Salzteig*, or salt dough, was given to a bridal couple by the bride's mother as a good luck charm. Its ingredients of flour, salt and water, represented the essentials for sustaining life, thus the household would never starve. The practice still continues today, but the modern gift consists of a loaf of bread and a bag of salt!

Salt dough was popular all over eastern Europe in the early nineteenth century, and peasants used to make salt-dough Christmas-tree decorations, adding a high percentage of salt to prevent them being eaten by rats.

My introduction to doughcraft was purely by chance. Four years ago, I was fascinated to see 'A Demonstration of Salt Dough Sculpture' being advertised on the programme of our local young wives group. I duly went along to the meeting with very little idea of what to expect. Since that day, I have been totally addicted to dough sculpture – as have the rest of my family, fortunately!

Everybody has creative ability, and immense satisfaction can be gained from producing a beautiful article. My passion for this medium grows almost daily, and I have obtained a great deal of pleasure from seeing other people's excitement as the projects grow before their eyes. Modelling dough is therapeutic and relaxing, as I have seen myself in workshops for the elderly, disabled people and children. Once you have mastered the basic techniques shown in the first chapter the designs are all easily assembled, and by varying, for example, the leaf type or flower used on a piece, you can bring a charming originality to your work.

Inspiration for designs can be drawn from a multitude of sources – objects around the home, in nature, art, pictures, wood carvings, pottery, etc. Your only limits are the bounds of your imagination. The projects chosen for this book all reflect a rural theme, and a wide variety of subjects ensures that there is something suitable for everyone. I hope that these designs will inspire you to try your hand at doughcraft, and that you will gain as much enjoyment from your baking as I do.

Opposite Fruit Basket (page 60), Vase of Roses (page 92),
Thatched Cottage (page 100), and Mice and Hedgehogs (page 26)

1
GETTING
STARTED

THE DOUGH

*T*he basic ingredients for salt dough couldn't be simpler.

1 **Good-quality plain flour** – poor-quality flour results in a poor dough texture.
2 **Fine-grain cooking or table salt** – a coarse grain gives a roughness to the dough which makes it harder to model.
3 **Water** – a smoother dough is achieved if the chill is taken off the water, as this helps to dissolve the grains of salt. However, take care that it is not warm, or the gluten in the flour will develop, making the dough elastic and difficult to handle.

There are several optional extras:

Vegetable oil or glycerine – a tablespoon of either of these may be added with the water to the basic dough mix. They give a slightly more pliable dough, but I find that the dough quickly forms a 'skin' and, during baking, remains a paler colour, not developing that lovely golden-brown colour associated with bread.

Wallpaper paste – a tablespoon of dry wallpaper paste may be added to the flour when making dough. This does not affect the consistency of the raw or cooked dough and it has the advantage of containing a mould inhibitor.

Cornflour or farine (potato flour) – a proportion of either of these may be substituted for the wheat flour. They do not contain gluten which gives flour its elasticity, and therefore they produce a stronger, tougher dough. This is good for very fine, detailed work, but the dough is harder to work with and not really suitable for the projects in this book. The dough is also much whiter than that made from wheat flour, and even when baked has an uncooked appearance.

PAINTS

Water-based paints are the best and easiest to use and can either be artists' water colours, poster paint, acrylic or gouache. They are all widely available from shops such as W. H. Smith as well as specialist art and craft shops.

Water colours can be bought in tubes or small cakes. They are a transparent colour and as such you will have to apply many layers to achieve an opaque finish. A gentle wash of colour is effective, though, if you want to preserve the natural look of the dough.

Poster paint may be used on dough models, but the range of colours is more limited than water colour or gouache and thus the colouring tends to be rather garish. The final texture may also be rather powdery.

Acrylic paint dries to a hard, plastic-like finish, helping to protect the dough from moisture, but remember to wash your brush and palette well before it dries or they will be ruined. This quick-drying quality can also make blending of colours tricky.

Gouache paint is more opaque than water colour but can be watered down to a delicate transparent wash. This makes it very versatile for use on salt-dough sculpture. Like water colour, gouache is available in a wide range of colours.

It is also possible to use spirit-based enamel paints, such as Humbrol. These can prove expensive as quite a large amount is generally required. As they are not water-based they must be thinned with a spirit solvent.

VARNISH

A good-quality, hard varnish is necessary to protect the finished dough article, the best being a clear polyurethane yacht varnish from your local DIY store. There are numerous specialist varnishes available from craft shops, but these tend to be expensive and they are often thin and watery, soaking into the dough rather than forming a waterproof coating.

TOOLS AND EQUIPMENT

The tools and equipment for dough making are readily found in the kitchen and very few specialist items are required. You will need:

1 **Rolling pin**
2 **Mixing bowl**
3 **Sharp knife**
4 **Baking sheets and round cake tins** – The salt in the dough will quickly attack the surface of the tins so causing them to rust. The non-stick variety are much hardier, but still not totally infallible! It is possible to cover them with foil or paper but these may stick and can prove expensive if you are making a lot of dough. If, however, you choose to do this, silicone baking parchment is the best. It is a good idea to set some old tins aside specifically for your dough, washing and drying them thoroughly after each use.
5 **Modelling tools** – All sorts of kitchen gadgets can be used for modelling and making patterns on the dough. No special tools are required but the most useful item is a thin wooden or bamboo skewer. A cocktail stick serves the same purpose, but it is not as strong and the extra length makes the skewer easier to handle. Scissors, forks, knives, pastry wheel, icing crimpers and paper-clips will also come in useful.

6 **Cutters** – All shapes and sizes of cutters are useful, particularly leaf and flower shapes, although they are not absolutely necessary, as these can be moulded by hand.
7 **Brushes** – A pastry brush or wide paint-brush is necessary for wetting the dough whilst you are assembling your models. For painting, synthetic brushes are preferable to sable or bristle as they are much harder wearing and both dough and acrylic paints are tough on brushes. A No 4 round brush for fine work, a No 7 for general painting and a 10mm ($\frac{3}{8}$in) flat brush for larger areas should be sufficient. For varnishing, a 38mm ($1\frac{1}{2}$in) brush is most suitable, but make sure it is of good quality so that your work doesn't end up covered in bristles!
8 **Potato ricer or garlic press** – These items are particularly useful as they make the most wonderful grass or hair, by extruding long strands of dough through the holes. For the uninitiated, a potato ricer is rather like a giant garlic press and is widely used in the catering industry for mashing potatoes. Both tools are available from good kitchen shops or catering suppliers, and also from certain mail-order companies such as 'Lakeland Plastics'.
9 **Cloves** – Invaluable for stalks and eyes!

MAKING DOUGH

*I*t is best to use a straight-sided mug to measure out your ingredients as this makes it easier to calculate quantities. The basic ratio of ingredients is two of flour, one of salt and one of water. For the projects using smaller quantities of dough, you may prefer to measure the water held by the mug in fluid ounces or millilitres, and then divide or multiply this. The table below should help provide a quick reckoning – but *do* add the water carefully and sparingly to avoid making the mixture too wet.

A dough mixture using four cupfuls of flour should be sufficient for a couple of large projects, such as a garland and basket; while a quantity of dough made with one cup of flour should be enough to make a small model, such as a collection of mushrooms or a selection of small animals.

Ratios of flour : salt : water (using a straight-sided mug)

Plain Flour	Salt	Water
4	2	2
3	$1\frac{1}{2}$	$1\frac{1}{2}$
2	1	1
1	$\frac{1}{2}$	$\frac{1}{2}$

Mix the flour and salt well, then add the water all in one go and knead well. An electric mixer with a dough hook or beater is ideal for this, if you have one large enough. The most important part of making dough sculptures is to get the consistency of the dough right. It should be firm yet pliable, somewhere between the consistencies of bread dough and short-crust pastry. A dough that is too dry will crumble and be difficult to work with; one that is too wet will be sticky to use and not hold its shape well. Different brands of flour absorb water to differing degrees, so you may need to be a little flexible with this recipe. It is always easy, however, to knead in a little more flour or water to change the consistency of the dough. Note, that a small difference in the amount of water added can change the consistency of the dough considerably, so add any extra sparingly. It may be sufficient just to wet your hands and re-knead the dough.

KNEADING

Once you have made your dough it is important to knead it really thoroughly for at least five minutes. Although an electric mixer is useful for making the dough, it is always best to give it a final kneading by hand. The warmth of your hands helps to give the dough elasticity and to combine the grains of salt, giving a smoother consistency.

STORING UNCOOKED DOUGH

I have read, and been told, that it is possible to store uncooked dough for some time, but I have never found this to be successful. Once the dough has been made up for more than a couple of hours it is difficult to use. It attracts moisture from the atmosphere and becomes sticky. The gluten in the flour develops, making the dough more elastic. This causes a reduction in sharpness of detail, as the dough does not hold its shape so well, once moulded.

If you do find it necessary to keep your dough, do not refrigerate but put it in a clean polythene bag. If left open to the air it will form a dry skin. It is generally quicker and easier to make a fresh batch than to battle on with inferior dough. Once moulded to the required design, it should go straight into the oven. If left out, it will form a dry skin which will crack and become unsightly once cooked.

MODELLING DOUGH

If your dough is the correct consistency it will be easy to work with. When rolling out dough, do so with a floured rolling pin on a floured surface, and treat it exactly as you would pastry.

When modelling by hand or rolling sausage shapes, it is best not to use flour. The dough will not stick to your hands and will be harder to shape if floured. You will find that you need to wash your hands frequently whilst modelling, so work close to a sink. The kitchen obviously makes the ideal workplace, and is usually of a suitable temperature. If it is too cold, the dough will be stiff; if too warm it may become too soft to work with.

It is best to work directly on to your baking sheet, as moving your model once it is finished may distort it. Grease the tray very lightly with vegetable oil, or use silicone parchment to line it.

JOINING DOUGH

When assembling your dough models, dampen the relevant area slightly with a little water to join together the component parts. Too much water will produce a slippery, rather than a sticky, surface and the pieces will tend to slide around.

Fresh dough can be used to join together or repair ready-baked or hardened pieces of dough. Or, mix fresh dough with water to form a thick starch paste which can then be brushed on to the surfaces to be joined. Similarly, holes or cracks can be filled with fresh dough. When the join is completed, if the piece has not been varnished, re-bake the dough on no more than 100°C (200°F/ Gas Mark $\frac{1}{4}$) for an hour or so. This will be sufficient as only the small amount of fresh dough will need to cook. If the dough has been varnished, leave the joins to dry at room temperature.

If any pieces of dough need supporting during baking, a scrunched up piece of tin foil will make a suitable prop placed underneath the piece. This can be removed once the dough is set hard.

USING TEMPLATES

Templates can be very useful in providing you with shapes for doughcraft designs, allowing you to achieve just the outline you want and making it easier to repeat the shape.

Actual-size templates for some of the projects in the book have been provided (see pages 118–26). To use, simply trace or photocopy the template on to thin card. Cut out the shape, lay lightly on top of the rolled out dough and cut around the outline using a sharp knife.

The templates may also be used to enlarge or reduce designs. In this case, the template will need to be enlarged or reduced using a photocopier. Remember, of course, that dough requirements will also vary with the size of the model.

BAKING DOUGH

The oven temperature should be 100–120°C (200–250°F/Gas Mark $\frac{1}{4}$–$\frac{1}{2}$). As a general rule of thumb it takes approximately one hour for every 6mm ($\frac{1}{4}$in) of dough thickness, but, as long as the temperature is no higher than 120°C (250°F/Gas Mark $\frac{1}{2}$), a longer time will do no harm. The drying out process will take several hours.

Once you have experimented and become familiar with how long models take to cook in your own oven, you may find it convenient to bake overnight. The temperature of the oven can always be lowered slightly to compensate for the longer cooking time.

Once cooked, your dough should be golden-brown and should lift easily from the tray. Press it underneath at the thickest part and make sure it is not at all soft. A quick tap on the underside should give a hollow sound. A dull sound will indicate that the dough in the centre is still soft, so it should be returned to the oven. It is most important that the dough is hard all the way through, as, if not, it will continue to dry out after varnishing and the model will shrink and crack. All ovens are different, so experiment with moving dough around in your oven to achieve the best results.

PAINTING DOUGH

Make sure the dough sculpture is quite cold before you begin to paint, as the painted surface will craze if it is still hot. Water-based paints can be thinned further with water to achieve different effects – thicker paints giving a bright, stunning effect; thinner paint producing a more subtle appearance. The most successful results are achieved using water-based paints quite thinly, giving a slightly transparent effect which is highly suitable for the projects in this book. A wide variety of colours are available in ready-to-use paints, but if you do not wish to purchase too many different colours you can mix your own from the basic primary colours, using the colour wheel below as a guide.

It is possible to colour your dough before baking, using spices, food colourings or powder paints, but these techniques do not lend themselves to the particular projects which follow.

If you want to leave your dough a natural colour, it is possible to add emphasis to the detail by giving the piece a wash of thin red/brown paint all over, creating a sepia effect. Alternatively, you may like to use an egg-wash to colour your model. A deeper golden glaze is particularly effective on a bread ring or wheatsheaf. Simply beat an egg with a tablespoon of water and brush on to the model before baking.

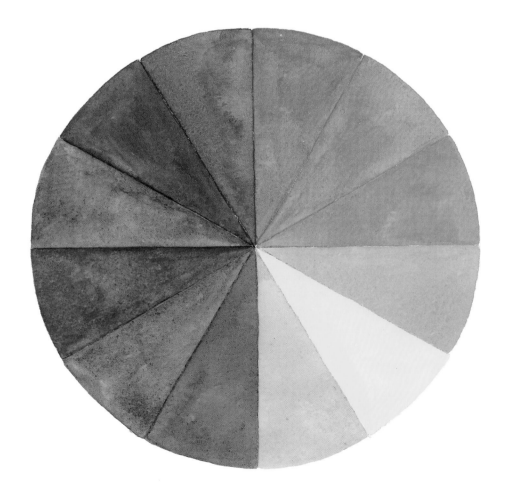

BASIC TECHNIQUES

VARNISHING DOUGH

This is probably the most important part in the production of your model, as it will live or die on the quality of the varnishing.

It is imperative that the paint is completely dry before you begin or you will trap moisture in your model which will cause the varnish to flake. Water-based paint does not take long to dry, and providing it does not feel at all damp to the touch, you are ready to varnish. If in doubt, pop your model back into a cool oven or place it on top of a radiator for a few minutes.

When varnishing, ensure that every nook and cranny is well covered, as even a pinhead-sized hole in the varnish will allow moisture through which may soften the dough. Give your pieces at least two but preferably three coats of varnish on both sides for maximum protection. It helps to wear disposable gloves to protect your hands when varnishing and that way you need not be cautious about getting good coverage. Varnish your piece all over in one go and leave it to dry on a wire rack, such as a cake cooling tray, for about six hours between coats. If you do not have a rack or something similar, you will need to varnish first the back of the article, and then, when that is dry, varnish the front, making sure that the varnish doesn't run through to the other side causing drips and runs. Place the model on a plastic sheet to dry. It will easily lift off plastic, whereas paper will stick to the varnish.

CARE OF DOUGHCRAFT MODELS

Under normal household conditions your dough should keep for many years. If kept in an excessively damp atmosphere it may soften, but it can be re-hardened (see Troubleshooting). To clean it, simply dust or wipe with a damp cloth.

After some time, you may find that a new coat of varnish will brighten it up. Do not place in direct steam such as over a kettle or in a steamy bathroom as this may affect the varnish. Direct sunlight should be avoided as it will fade the paint.

HANGERS

There are three basic ways to hang your dough on the wall.

HOLES
This method is suitable for smallish, fairly flat pieces of dough. Do not poke a hole in your piece with a skewer, as this may distort the shape and could close up in baking. It is better to cut a piece out, using a strong plastic drinking straw as a miniature cutter.

RIBBONS
With a piece such as a basket, you can tie a ribbon around the handle, forming a loop to hang the model by and a decorative bow. Thin ribbon can also be threaded through holes made in the dough.

HOOKS
A metal hook can be pushed into the raw dough and then baked in the model. As the dough cooks it will swell slightly and mould itself around the hook, finally hardening and holding it in place. Hooks can be made from twisted pieces of florists' wire, hair pins, or even loops of string, but by far the most convenient method is to use a suitably sized paper-clip. Make absolutely sure it is large enough to penetrate well into the dough. Small paper-clips are only suitable for the smallest projects, most will need at least a 38mm ($1\frac{1}{2}$in) size clip. The giant, wavy clips, available from stationers or office suppliers, are the most suitable for the larger projects. Try to make sure that when you push your hanger into your dough model it will hang straight on the wall. This involves a certain amount of guesswork, but with a little practice you will soon be able to judge the centre of gravity perfectly.

Having mastered the basic techniques, you are all set to start creating your own beautiful models. If things should go wrong, don't despair – most problems are easily solved. The following is a list of the more common faults that may occur.

RISING, BLISTERING DOUGH

If the dough rises and forms bubbles during baking, this is an indication that either the dough was too wet or the oven too hot – or both! If the dough is still soft enough, pierce the bubbles with a pin and gently press back into shape. Reduce the temperature of the oven for the remainder of the cooking time. For future reference, if the dough is too soft it will not hold its shape well and detail will be lost. If the oven is too hot, the dough will start to brown slightly before it hardens. This should help you decide what caused the fault and how to avoid it next time.

CRACKS

It seems that cracks which appear during or after baking are an occupational hazard. Although they are rare, sometimes it is almost impossible to avoid them. Cracks on the reverse of your model are incidental to the baking process and are not detrimental in any way to the piece. These are the sort of breaks that you find in 'real bread'. They appear more in thicker models, and can be some-what avoided by cooking at a lower temperature.

The cracks that are particularly upsetting are the hairline cracks that appear from nowhere after baking is complete. Changes of temperature cause slight expansion and contraction in the baked dough, causing stresses which can lead to cracking. Sometimes this happens during the cooling process, particularly with larger pieces, so it helps to cool them very slowly in the oven, gradually reducing the temperature until the oven is switched off. Leave the model in the oven until completely cool.

Another method which reduces the incidence of cracking, particularly in the larger pieces, is the same as that used for reinforcing concrete. Build the base of your model up in layers, inserting a piece of nylon tulle netting (available from any fabric shop) between the layers. Full instructions for this are given in Chapter 7 on wall plaques.

If cracks do appear after baking they can be filled with a little fresh dough using the same principle as a filler on plaster. If the model is already painted and varnished, leave the filler dough to dry out naturally in a warm room, and, when dry, touch up with fresh paint and varnish. It is not advisable to re-bake, as the changes in temperature may cause another crack!

SOFTENING DOUGH

If atmospheric conditions are exceptionally humid, or your dough models are kept in an excessively damp atmosphere, they may become soft and spongy. They can be re-hardened by placing them on a radiator or in the airing cupboard for several days. Alternatively, they may be placed in a cool oven (no more than $100°C/200°F/$Gas Mark $\frac{1}{4}$) for 2–3 hours. This will darken the varnish slightly and will smell dreadful but will not harm your model in any way! If the varnish shows any sign of bubbling it means that the oven is too hot.

REPAIRING BREAKAGES

Salt dough is fairly durable but will break if dropped. If the break is clean and your model is not in too many pieces it can be repaired very successfully with superglue or a resin-based adhesive which works with a hardener, such as 'Araldite'.

If the damage is small, such as an ear knocked off and lost, or the end of a leaf crumbled away, the offending part of the model can be restructured using fresh dough. Leave to dry in a warm place before retouching with paint and varnish.

FLAKING VARNISH

This is caused by damp or steam. The appearance of your sculpture can be improved by rubbing away the flaking varnish with a rough cloth, such as towelling, or, gently, with a very fine piece of emery paper, taking care not to scratch the paint underneath. Then give two coats of fresh varnish and re-hang in a drier location.

CREATING BASIC SHAPES

Mastering certain basic shapes, such as fruits, flowers, vegetables, leaves, breads and so on, will allow you not only to produce the wide variety of designs in this book, but to create your own original models.

Begin by rolling out the dough exactly as you would pastry, using a floured rolling pin on a lightly floured surface. Flat shapes can be cut using pastry cutters or a sharp knife. If necessary, use a cardboard template by tracing the patterns at the back of the book (see pages 118–26). Other shapes are moulded by hand.

FRUIT

STRAWBERRIES
A small ball of dough, moulded to a point at one end and marked with a cocktail stick to give the effect of the seeds. For the stalk use a de-seeded clove, or cut a small star-shaped leaf from a small flattened ball of dough, and anchor this in place with a clove stalk.

PEAR
A ball of dough, elongated and narrowed at one end, with a clove stalk as in the apple, and a small leaf added.

GRAPES
Small balls of dough arranged in a slight 'S' shape. Add leaf, stalk and vine – a spaghetti-shaped piece of dough laid on top and twisted.

APPLE
A simple ball of dough with a clove pushed in 'head-first' to make a stalk. A leaf can be added if required.

PLUMS
A small oval-shaped ball of dough, with a crease added down one side using a cocktail stick, and a hole pressed in the top. Size, shape and colour can be varied to produce cherries, peaches, apricots, etc.

ORANGE
A ball of dough 'pitted' with the blunt end of a bamboo skewer, or rolled on the zesting part of a cheese grater to give the orange peel effect. A clove with the seed broken off is used as the stalk.

BANANAS
Are best avoided!

FLOWERS

DAHLIA, MARIGOLD, CHRYSANTHEMUM

A stylised version of any of these can be made by placing a round ball of dough on top of a flattened piece and then snipping all the way round both pieces of dough with a small pair of scissors.

DAFFODIL

Assemble outer petals from flattened, elongated pieces of dough. The centre is made from a small, sausage-shaped piece, flattened and then rolled up and placed on top of the outer petals.

PANSY

Five petals made from flattened balls of dough, slightly pointed at one end and assembled as shown in the photograph. Push a hole in the centre with a skewer or cocktail stick.

DAISY SHAPE

This can be made from thinly rolled out dough using a small sugarcraft cutter, or moulded from a small, flattened ball of dough with the edges drawn up with a cocktail stick. Push a hole in the centre.

ROSE

The centre of the rose is made from a flattened ball of dough rolled up to form a tight bud. The flower is built up to the required shape by rolling successive flattened dough petals around the centre bud.

LEAVES

*L*eaves of different shapes and sizes can easily be made either by moulding or cutting.

USING CUTTERS

This method is especially useful for leaves of complicated shape such as holly or ivy. Roll dough out thinly with a rolling pin and, after using the cutter, mark veins with a cocktail stick.

PINCHED LEAVES

A stylised leaf suitable for trees or hedges can be made by pinching a piece of dough between thumb and forefinger, then breaking it off. Make a number, then pile them on top of each other.

CUT LEAVES

A simple leaf can be made from a rolled out piece of dough, by cutting it into long narrow strips and then cutting these into diamond shapes. Veins are marked with a cocktail stick.

MOULDED LEAVES

These can be made from a flattened ball of dough pinched to a point at one end. The sides can be drawn up with a skewer if desired to give more of an oak leaf effect. Mark veins as before.

CAULIFLOWER

As for the cabbage, but with a larger centre ball and fewer outside leaves. Pit the centre with the blunt end of a bamboo skewer, then, using the point, or a cocktail stick, divide the cauliflower head into florets.

POTATO

Roll oval-shaped balls of dough and, using the blunt end of a wooden skewer, mark three or four 'eyes' in each potato. They will look very realistic when painted.

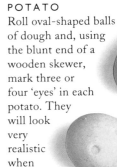

GREEN BEANS

Roll a long thin piece of dough, thinnest at the very end, and flatten roughly, making indentations with your thumb at regular intervals.

LEEK

Flatten a long sausage of dough at one end, then cut off that end in a 'V' shape. Add roots made from dough extruded through a garlic press and mark the leaves

with a sharp knife. The best effect can be seen when painted.

CARROT

Roll a long pointed piece of dough, and then, using a very small circular cutter or the end of a piping tube, mark a ring in the top of the carrot. Using a sharp knife, mark fine ridges across the carrot all the way down it.

TOMATOES

Make a small ball of dough, adding a star-shaped leaf held with a clove 'stalk' as for a strawberry.

MUSHROOMS

Roll a small ball of dough, and using a very small circular cutter or the end of a piping nozzle, press about halfway into the dough to form the stalk.

ASPARAGUS

Roll a bundle of spear-shaped pieces of dough and snip the ends and shafts with nail scissors.

CABBAGE

Using a ball of dough for the centre of the cabbage, build up the outside leaves in the same way as you add the petals when making a rose.

*T*ree trunks can be formed by the following methods, with leaves and fruit added.

A long roll of dough, flattened slightly, and the bark marked with a knife.

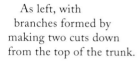

As left, with branches formed by making two cuts down from the top of the trunk.

As right, but with two thinner versions twisted together.

A long sausage of dough, twisted slightly and pinched in places to give a gnarled appearance.

The base of a tree trunk needs to be finished off to give a neat appearance. Either spread the base out slightly and add extruded dough 'grass', or plant it in a dough pot!

The scope here is endless, as you will realise if you have visited a good continental bakery. Poppy seeds, sesame seeds, rolled oats, and many other types of grains or seeds can be sprinkled on to add interest, but be sure to brush the top of your dough with water first or they won't stick. Bread rolls also make a good subject for fridge magnets. The following are a few examples of rolls that are easy to make.

FRENCH STICK
A long thin sausage of dough, marked with diagonal cuts across the top.

BLOOMER
A shorter, fatter version of the French stick.

COTTAGE LOAF
A small slightly flattened ball of dough placed on top of a larger one. Push a hole through the centre and mark lines with a knife all round.

SESAME SEED BUNS
Traditional round burger buns.

KNOT
Made from a long sausage of dough, thinner at the ends and wrapped in a simple knot, this looks attractive when sprinkled with poppy seeds.

GRANARY LOAF
This can be shaped from dough made with wholemeal flour to give it texture.

COBURG
A basic round loaf with a cross cut in the top.

BREAD ROLLS

PLAIT WITH POPPY SEEDS

Traditional plait constructed from three sausage shapes, thinner at the ends. Your rolls of dough need to be twice as long as you require the finished plait to be.

SLICED LOAF

Form dough into a basic oblong shape, then using a sharp knife and a sawing motion, cut the slices from this fun loaf, leaving slices attached at the base so that they bend over as shown in the photograph.

PRETZEL

Made from a long roll of dough thinned out at each end.

FEATHERS AND SPINES

Feathers can easily be marked on a wing-shaped piece of dough, using the end of a paper-clip.

Snipping with scissors also produces a feather-like effect (particularly suitable for owls). The cuts can be made in different sizes to give the effect of hedgehog spines, flower petals or ears of wheat.

Extruded dough, pushed through a potato ricer, or garlic press, makes wonderful 'hair'. This can be cut off with a knife to different lengths to make grass, hair, sheep's wool, manes and tails, etc.

*G*arlands are a very popular subject for salt-dough models and can be formed in a variety of ways.

It is essential to keep your garlands perfectly round (assuming that you are making a circular wreath) as any misshaping will spoil the effect.

The best way to do this is to use a round baking sheet, for example a 'pizza-tray' or an upturned cake tin, of approximately the size that you wish your finished garland to be. By working directly on to this round tin and following the outline of it, you preserve the shape perfectly.

FLAT CUT-OUT GARLAND
This can be made by rolling out dough to approximately 13mm (½in) thick and then choosing two round objects of suitable size, one slightly larger than the other – for example, a saucer and a tea-plate. Place the larger plate on your dough and cut round it using a sharp knife, then, ensuring the smaller plate is central, cut round that. This will result in a hollow, perfectly circular ring which can then be used as a base for your fruit, flowers etc.

GARLANDS WITH LEAVES
Roll out a long 'snake' of dough and place it around a circular tin, about 25mm (1in) from the edge, ensuring that you leave enough space around the edge for the leaves. Press the two ends together to form a ring. Then make the leaves from flattened balls of dough following the instructions on page 17. Brush your ring with water (a paint-brush is the best tool for this), then simply place the leaves around the dough ring, pressing them lightly into position.

TWISTED GARLAND
This is made from two long rolls of dough. Before rolling your dough give it an extra knead to ensure a good smooth finish. Roll out two 'snakes' of dough approximately 19mm (¾in) thick and place them side by side. As a general guide their length should be three times the diameter of your baking tin.

With the two pieces side by side, roll them together into a twist, taking care to keep the twists even along the length of the dough. Place the twisted length on your tin, around the edge of the circle. Join by cutting the two ends diagonally, moistening with water and pressing together.

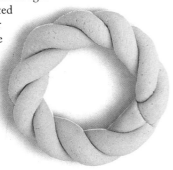

PLAITED GARLAND
This is formed in the same way as the twisted garland but using three rolls of dough plaited together. Roll out three long snakes of dough, their length three times the diameter of your tin, and plait together, taking care to keep the shape of the plait even. A good way to prevent the plait from becoming thick at one end and thin at the other, is to start plaiting at the centre and work out towards the ends. Place on a round baking tray and join as for the twisted garland.

$\mathscr{D}$ough baskets can be fashioned in many different ways, and be either wall-hanging or free-standing. The projects in this book use basic flat wall-hanging baskets in different shapes and with different types of weave.

BASKET-WEAVE EFFECTS

1 A simple basket-weave pattern can be created using a wooden skewer to press lines into the dough.

2 A much finer 'weave' can be created using a fork to make the evenly spaced lines across the basket, with a wooden skewer drawn down over them to form the vertical lines.

3 Baskets can be woven from thin strips of dough. Roll your dough out to 6mm ($\frac{1}{4}$in) thick and using the straight edge of a ruler to guide your knife, cut strips of dough approximately 13mm ($\frac{1}{2}$in) wide. Then, attach the vertical strips to your basket base using a little water and carefully weave the horizontal strips through. Trim off the edges neatly with a knife when you have finished. A small twist of dough at the bottom adds the finishing touch.

4 Another basket-weave effect can be achieved using icing crimpers, a useful tool for dough making and readily available from kitchen shops. Simply pinch the crimpers together in vertical lines down the basket. The same effect can be achieved by pressing the prongs of a fork into the dough in one direction and then the other.

5 An overlapping style of basket can be created by building up a layer of over-lapping strips on top of a rolled out base. It is particularly suitable for larger projects where a more substantial basket is required.

BASKET HANDLES

Basket handles are produced by rolling out long snakes of dough, twisting them together, then attaching to the basic basket shape using a little water on the joins. To finish off, attach a small twist at the base of your basket to act as a pedestal.

To make any of the baskets in this book, roll out a sheet of dough 10mm ($\frac{3}{8}$in) thick and cut to shape from one of the many templates found in the back of the book (see pages 120–22).

2
ANIMALS

MICE AND HEDGEHOGS

These cute little animals are the simplest of all the projects and can be made in a few minutes. The ideal size is about 51–76mm (2–3in) long, but it is fun to make families of them in a variety of sizes. Although the little creatures in the photographs are left in the natural dough finish, you can also paint them to give variety.

To make the mice and hedgehogs shown you will need:

- *2 cups flour made into dough (see page 11)*
- *Wooden skewer or cocktail stick*
- *Black-headed map pins or cloves*
- *Small, pointed scissors*
- *Varnish*

MOUSE

1 Take a ball of dough of the size you want your mouse to be and roll it smoothly. Roll one end between the palms of your hands to give the conical shape of the mouse's pointed nose. Lay dough on a baking tray.

2 Make two ears from small balls of dough, flattened between the fingers and pinched together at the base. Dampen and attach these to the mouse's body, towards the nose. Mark eyes with a skewer or cocktail stick. Roll a long piece of 'spaghetti' dough, tuck one end under its bottom and bring the rest of the tail up over the mouse's body, curling it round – the dough is not strong enough to leave the tail sticking out.

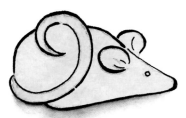

3 Bake, then varnish as instructed in Basic Techniques.

HEDGEHOG

1 Follow step 1 as for the mouse.

2 Holding the body in the palm of one hand, using small, sharp scissors, snip spines all over the body beginning about 10mm ($\frac{3}{8}$in) from the nose. Work diagonally across the body to avoid cutting the spines in rows – this would be obvious on the finished piece. Mark the eyes with a cocktail stick or skewer and push a black-headed map pin into the end of the nose. If you haven't one of these, an ordinary black glass-headed dressmakers' pin will suffice, or, failing that, a small clove.

3 Bake and varnish as instructed in Basic Techniques.

SITTING AND LYING CATS

These rather comical ginger toms are quite simply made, and, as with the mice and hedgehogs, are rather fun in families. Why not try a mother cat with an assortment of different coloured kittens?

To make both cats you will need:
- *2 cups flour made into dough (see page 11)*
- *Wooden skewer or cocktail stick*
- *Black-headed map pins*
- *Paper-clips*
- *Paint*
- *Varnish*

LYING CAT

1 Roll a smooth golf-ball-sized ball of dough and flatten it slightly for the body. Add two small pea-sized balls of dough for the paws.

2 Add a smaller, slightly flattened ball of dough for the head, and pinch two small pieces of dough between thumb and forefinger, to form the ears. Dampen the base of the ears and attach to the top of the head. For the facial detail, add two small flattened balls of dough for the cheeks and a black-headed map pin for the nose. Mark the whiskers and eyes using a cocktail stick or wooden skewer.

3 Finally, add a long sausage of dough, pointed at one end and slip it under the body at the back curling it round to form the tail. Mark claws in the paws with a cocktail stick.

4 Bake, paint as desired and varnish as instructed in Basic Techniques.

SITTING CAT

1 Form the body and head as for the lying cat. Attach together and add facial details as shown below.

2 Add rolls of dough for legs, with a small ball of dough at the base of each leg for the paws. Mark the claws as before.

3 Finally, add a tail as shown.

4 Push a small paper-clip into the ball of the head to form a hanger. Bake, paint as desired and varnish as instructed in Basic Techniques. Cats can be painted in any colour – a stripey cat is very effective, as shown in the photograph.

DUCK AND DUCKLINGS

Ducks are an ever popular subject, and these would be equally suitable for kitchen, bathroom or a child's bedroom. They can be made and displayed individually or as a group. Why not try three ducks flying across the wall?

The mother duck and ducklings are made in the same way but in different sizes.

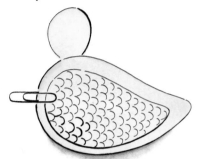

1 To make each duckling take a piece of dough the size of a golf ball, and roll it into a smooth cone shape. Press flat and lay on baking tray. Repeat with a slightly smaller piece of dough for the wing, marking the feathers with the end of a paper-clip. Lay this on top of the body.

2 With a little water, attach an egg-shaped piece of dough, approximately the size of a grape for the head. Form a small cone of dough for the beak and snip the pointed end open with the scissors. Moisten and attach to the front of the head.

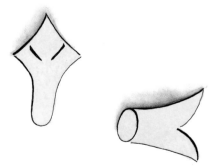

3 For the feet, make a small thin cone of dough, flatten and shape the end to a point with your fingers. Moisten the top end of the foot, and lifting the body gently, slip it underneath. Mark the foot webbing with a cocktail stick or skewer.

To make the complete group you will need:

- *2 cups flour made into dough (see page 11)*
- *Wooden skewer or cocktail stick*
- *Cloves*
- *Scissors*
- *Paper-clips*
- *Paint*
- *Varnish*

4 Add the bow by placing two small triangles of dough, pointed ends together, at the duckling's neck, as shown. The ribbons hanging from the bow are painted on to the chest after baking. Mark the eye with a skewer. Lastly, push a small paper-clip well into the dough just behind the head for the hanging ribbon.

5 To make the mother duck, use an orange-sized ball of dough for the body, and increase the other pieces correspondingly. Use a clove for the eye and add two feet instead of one.

6 Cut two long thin triangles of flattened dough for the ribbons at mother duck's neck and attach these to the body, thin ends touching the bow as shown.

7 Bake, paint beaks and feet yellow, and bows and ribbons in the colour of your choice. Varnish as instructed in Basic Techniques.

*T*hese delightful pigs are made by combining the skills of rolling and cutting dough with hand modelling. The pigs can be left plain, or painted to give a 'spotty' effect, or even painted pink for fun. A thick black marking pen makes easy work of adding spots. If you require a darker finish to your dough, for example for a brown pig or a saddleback, turn the oven up to 150°C (300°F/Gas Mark 2) for about 1 hour after baking is complete, or add some brown spice, powder paint, or food colouring to the raw dough.

To make all these pigs you will need:

- *2 cups flour made into dough (see page 11)*
- *Wooden skewer or cocktail stick*
- *Sharp knife*
- *Paper-clips*
- *Paint*
- *Varnish*

LARGE AND SMALL PIGS

1 Roll out half your dough to approximately 6mm (¼in) thick and using the trace-off templates (see page 118), cut out the basic shape your require. To form the body of the pig, roll a slightly oval ball of dough and flatten it. Dampen the base and lay the body on the top half, completely covering the upper edge. Roll a smaller ball of dough and flatten for the head, dampen and attach to body.

2 For the features, add a small ball of dough for the nose and press a slight hollow in it, using something like the blunt end of a pencil or the handle of a wooden spoon. Mark the eyes and nostrils with a skewer or cocktail stick. For the ears, roll two small sausages of dough, flatten them and attach with a little water to the top of the head as shown, bending them over to lie on the face.

3 Add a small curly tail and mark the legs and trotters with a knife. The larger size pig looks more realistic if you cut away some of the dough to form the legs. Push a paper-clip into the top for hanging, and position slightly towards the head of the pig so that he doesn't do a nose-dive when you hang him on the wall!

4 Bake, paint as desired and varnish as instructed in Basic Techniques.

MOTHER PIG AND PIGLETS

1 These are made in exactly the same way as the single pig, but instead of legs we add piglets! Use the correct template at the back of the book (see page 118). Note, that the template for the base of the mother pig is much shorter than the standing pig because she is lying down.

2 Proceed as for the single pig as far as step 3. Then add two sausage-shaped front legs and mark the trotters with a knife.

3 Add the piglets by dampening the base and laying four small balls of dough against the mother's belly. The 'creases' are made with a wooden skewer or cocktail stick, and a small piece of spaghetti dough is attached to each to give a curly little tail!

4 Push a paper-clip into the top for hanging. Bake, paint as desired and varnish as instructed in Basic Techniques.

SHEEP FAMILY

This family of ewe, ram and woolly lambs are great fun to make and, although simple, provide very effective results. Children particularly love making the woolly bits!

To make the complete sheep family you will need:

- *3 cups flour made into dough (see page 11)*
- *Knife*
- *Potato ricer (preferably) or garlic press*
- *Wooden skewer or cocktail stick*
- *Cloves*
- *Paper-clips*
- *Paint*
- *Varnish*

1 Roll an oval ball of dough and flatten for the body. Take a smaller piece for the head and make it slightly pointed at the mouth. Dampen and attach to the body.

2 To make the legs, roll out a long thin sausage of dough, cut off the required length, fold in half and attach to the body as shown. Mark the feet with a knife. If you are making a ram, add horns made from a rolled up sausage of dough.

3 This is the fun part. Using a potato ricer (this is a very labour intensive process with a garlic press), make a heap of extruded dough cut off at approximately 19mm ($\frac{3}{4}$in) long. Brush the body with water and attach the wool all over, not forgetting the top of the head.

4 Add pointed ears, sticking out sideways not upwards, in front of the horns if you have them. Lastly, mark the eyes and nostrils with a wooden skewer or cocktail stick. Cloves can be used for eyes on the bigger sheep.

5 Add a paper-clip for hanging, estimating the centre of gravity to ensure your sheep hangs correctly. Bake, paint as desired and varnish as instructed in Basic Techniques.

TEDDY BEAR AND RABBIT

These two delightful figures make lovely decorations for a children's room. The teddy is designed along the lines of a traditional jointed bear, and the rabbit was inspired by Beatrix Potter's 'Flopsy Bunnies'.

For each of these animals you will need:

- *1 cup flour made into dough (see page 11)*
- *Wooden skewer or cocktail stick*
- *Black-headed map pins or cloves*
- *Sharp knife*
- *Paper-clip*
- *Paint*
- *Varnish*

TEDDY BEAR

1 Roll a smooth oval ball of dough for the body, dampen and add a smaller round ball for the head, then add an even smaller one for the muzzle.

2 Add sausages of dough for the arms and legs, shaping the legs a little as you roll them. The pads are marked with a skewer or cocktail stick. (The

ones on the feet can be marked by pressing the end of a piping nozzle into the dough, if you have one of suitable size.)

3 Add ears made from small balls of dough flattened between thumb and forefinger and pinched together at the base. The eyes and nose are map pins or cloves. Mark the mouth and a navel with a skewer and add a dough bow with ribbons at the neck.

4 Push a paper-clip into the top of the head for hanging. Bake, paint as desired and varnish according to instructions in Basic Techniques.

RABBIT

1 The head and body of the rabbit are made from two flattened pear-shaped pieces of dough, joined together with water.

2 Two sausage-shaped hind legs are added, one slipped under the body, the other laid on top. A smaller sausage is added for the arm and a ball of dough, roughened with a sharp knife, for the tail.

3 For the facial detail, add two long, pointed ears, moistened and firmly attached to the top of the head. Use a map pin for the nose, a clove for the eye and mark whiskers with the point of a sharp knife.

4 Finally add a bow at the neck as for the teddy and a paper-clip for hanging. Bake, paint and varnish as instructed in Basic Techniques.

FROGS AND OWLS

Many people are collectors of frogs or owls, and one of these little comic characters would make a lovely gift. Frogs are quite a difficult subject to model, but this very simple, stylised version, designed by my friend Linda Allen, is really quite easy to make. To add interest, you can sit him on a dough lily pad – a group of them together can look quite hilarious. You almost expect them to start hopping across the room!

To make a collection of animals you will need:

- *1 cup flour made into dough (see page 11)*
- *Black-headed map pins*
- *Sharp knife*
- *Small pointed scissors*
- *Paper-clips*
- *Paint*
- *Varnish*

FROG

1 Make an oval-shaped body and add a small ball of dough for the head. Try to blend the dough together so that the join doesn't show too much.

2 To add facial detail, use thumb and forefinger to pinch up the dough to form the eye recesses. Push in two map pins for eyes. Mark the nostrils and a nice wide smiley mouth with a skewer or cocktail stick.

3 Lift the body slightly and slip under two little front feet made from flattened dough sausages. For the hind legs, add two long thin rolls, meeting at the back of the body and brought round to the front, ending in flattened feet! Cut the toes with a knife.

4 Bake, paint as desired and varnish according to the instructions in Basic Techniques.

OWL

1 Make an inverted pear-shaped ball of dough and flatten it slightly for the owl body. Pinch the top corners between thumb and forefinger to form the ears. You may need to fiddle around a little to achieve just the right shape. Add two small, thin, flattened inverted tear-drop shapes for the wings, and either mark the feathers with the loop of a paper-clip or snip with scissors. Dot in the breast feathers with a skewer or cocktail stick and mark the tail feathers with a knife.

2 Add two eyes made from flattened balls of dough. Push a hole in the centre of each eye and mark 'bicycle spoke' lines around with a knife. Place a small triangular beak between the eyes.

3 Add two small, flattened triangular feet and mark the claws with a cocktail stick.

4 Add a paper-clip at the head for hanging. Bake, paint as desired and varnish according to the instructions in Basic Techniques.

COW AND PONY

$\mathcal{P}$onies are firm favourites with children, and this one was designed at the request of my horse-obsessed daughters! The cow is of the same basic construction and both animals can be painted in a variety of different colours to depict different breeds.

To make a cow and pony you will need:
- *2 cups flour made into dough (see page 11)*
- *Cloves*
- *Garlic press or potato ricer*
- *Wooden skewer or cocktail stick*
- *Paper-clips*
- *Paint*
- *Varnish*

COW

1 Roll out a fat sausage of dough and flatten it to form the body. Pinch one of the top corners into a point to form the prominent hip bone. Using the first two fingers of your right hand (assuming that you are right-handed), working against the palm of your left hand, roll out a thin piece of dough for each of the legs. Where your two fingers come together, the dough will naturally form a lump which makes a perfect knee joint. Slip the first two legs underneath the body.

2 Add a small ball of dough for the udder and then two more legs, this time attached to the top of the body with a little water. Roll a long, thin piece of dough with a wider piece at one end for the tail and attach to the cow's rear, making sure that the tail touches the body and legs all the way down as it will break if left sticking out.

3 Make an inverted pear shape for the head. Moisten it and attach to the body. Add pointed ears sticking out at right angles to the head.

4 Finally, add a pinched piece of dough for the top knot, cloves for eyes and mark nostrils with a

wooden skewer. Using a knife, make hair marks in the top knot and end of the tail.

5 Push a paper-clip hanger into the back of the cow, trying to ensure that it will hang straight once baked. It takes a certain amount of guesswork initially to find the centre of gravity, but with a little practice you will soon get it perfect. Bake, paint and varnish as instructed in Basic Techniques.

PONY

1 Form the body in the same way as the cow but without the prominent pelvic bone and with a more elongated neck.

2 Add the legs as for the cow, omitting the udder! Place an inverted pear-shaped head at the top of the neck.

3 Using dough extruded through a potato ricer or garlic press, add a long tail and a mane all the way down the neck. A small fringe of extruded dough forms the forelock.

4 Make the ears, which are smaller than the cow's and pointing upwards, and attach with a little water. Nostrils are made with a wooden skewer and cloves added for eyes.

5 Push a paper-clip hanger into the back of the pony, then bake, paint and varnish as instructed in Basic Techniques.

3
GARLANDS

FRUIT TWIST AND GRAPE RING

These are the simplest garlands – very quick and easy to produce. The grapes can be painted in almost any colour without looking odd, which is useful if you want to match a particular colour scheme.

To make two of these small garlands you will need:

- *2 cups flour made into dough (see page 11)*
- *Knife*
- *Cloves*
- *Baking tin 152–203mm (6–8in) diameter*
- *Paper-clips*
- *Paint*
- *Varnish*

FRUIT TWIST

I Following the instructions in Basic Techniques, make a small twisted garland, keeping about 19mm (³⁄₄in) inside the outer edge of your baking tin. Place three cut leaves over the join in the garland and then add an apple and pear.

2 Fill in the spaces round the apple and pear with plums and currants.

3 Add a paper-clip hanger directly opposite the fruit, taking care to bury it well in the dough but not pushing it right through. Bake, paint as desired and varnish.

GRAPE RING

I Form the twisted garland in the same way as for the Fruit Twist, but this time with the join at the top of the garland. Add three moulded leaves to cover this join.

2 Make a large bundle of small balls of dough for the grapes and, after moistening the garland, lift them into place to cascade down the side. Add a couple of pieces of spaghetti dough twisted to look like vines.

3 Add a paper-clip hanger and then bake, paint as desired and varnish.

FRUIT AND VEGETABLE GARLANDS

These traditional garlands make perfect kitchen decorations. They can be made in varying sizes to suit your requirements – simply add more or less fruit to the basic garland as shown in the photographs.

For a larger size garland you will need:

- *2 cups flour made into dough (see page 11)*
- *Wooden skewer or cocktail stick*
- *Cloves*
- *Baking tin 230mm (9in) diameter*
- *Paper-clip*
- *Paint*
- *Varnish*

FRUIT GARLAND

1 Following the instructions in Basic Techniques, lay a long sausage of dough around a circular baking tin and flatten slightly. Roll twelve balls of dough and flatten into leaves. Mark veins with a skewer and place on top of the dough circle.

2 Add two pears, two apples and two oranges as shown in the diagram. Then place two moulded leaves, five strawberries and a strawberry flower to the left of the main bunch of fruit, and a moulded leaf and a bunch of grapes to the right. Fill in any spaces between the fruits with plums and blackcurrants.

3 Push a very large paper-clip hanger into the top of the garland. Bake, paint as desired and varnish as instructed in Basic Techniques.

For the smaller garlands use a 178mm (7in) diameter baking tin and make a garland with nine leaves. Add fewer fruit and vegetables, as shown in the photographs.

VEGETABLE GARLAND

1 Proceed as for step 1 in the Fruit Garland.

2 Add the cauliflower, cabbage and potatoes (made as instructed in Basic Techniques) at the bottom of the garland, as shown in the diagram. The reason for this is that whilst the fruit needs to be at the top so that the bunch of grapes can hang downwards, the leeks and carrots look better growing upwards!

3 Place a bunch of leeks to one side of these vegetables and a bunch of carrots to the other. Finally, fill in any spaces with mushrooms and tomatoes. When you arrange your vegetables, bear in mind their colours when finished, and don't put items of the same or similar colours, such as leeks and cauliflower or tomatoes and carrots, next to each other.

4 Push a very large paper-clip hanger into the top of your garland. Bake, paint and varnish as instructed in Basic Techniques.

ROSE GARLAND

This variation of the garland makes a very pretty alternative for a bedroom or living room. The roses can be painted to match your decor and can be added singly or in clusters, depending on the size of garland your require.

The large and small garlands are made in the same way, with extra roses for the larger version

For the large rose garland you will need:
- *2 cups flour made into dough (see page 11)*
- *Wooden skewer or cocktail stick*
- *Baking tin 230mm (9in) diameter*
- *Paper-clip*
- *Paint*
- *Varnish*

1 Form a circular garland with leaves on your baking sheet using twelve balls of dough flattened into leaves approximately 50mm (2in) in diameter, following the instructions in Basic Techniques.

2 Form nine slightly smaller leaves with pointed ends and arrange on the garland as shown.

3 Form nine full-blown roses each approximately 25mm (1in) across, using the method explained in Basic Techniques. Lay these in a cluster, placing each rose between the rose leaves as shown. Add nine buds, made by rolling one or two petals tightly, placing one between each rose.

4 Push a large paper-clip into the top of your garland directly opposite the centre group of roses. Bake, paint in colours of your choice and varnish as instructed in Basic Techniques.

For the smaller size garland use a 178mm (7in) diameter baking tin and place nine leaves around the garland. Add one full-blown rose and three buds to each group of rose leaves.

PLAITED GARLAND

This garland is more intricate than those with the leaves, and the result is more delicate. Take care when painting this project, and use a small brush for the tiny berries and flowers.

To make this garland you will need:

- *2 cups flour made into dough (see page 11)*
- *Wooden skewer or cocktail stick*
- *Cloves*
- *Baking tin 230mm (9in) diameter*
- *Large paper-clip*
- *Paint*
- *Varnish*

1 Make a plaited garland as instructed in Basic Techniques, and place six leaves at the join at the bottom, as shown in the diagram.

2 Add an apple, orange and pear in the centre of this group of leaves, then place a cluster of strawberries to one side and plums to the other.

3 Fill in the spaces between the fruits with currants, and then place small leaves, small flowers and currants, either singly or in twos and threes, all round the garland, tucking them in between the ropes of the plait.

4 Push a large paper-clip for hanging into the garland opposite the main bunch of fruit, taking care that it does not pierce right through the dough. Bake, paint as desired and varnish as instructed in Basic Techniques.

BREAD AND WHEAT RING

*F*or obvious reasons salt dough lends itself wonderfully to the modelling of bread. Adding a few ears of wheat and the odd leaf lightens this garland and makes a superb kitchen decoration, particularly attractive at harvest time.

To make this garland you will need:

- *3 cups flour made into dough (see page 11)*
- *Cloves*
- *Small scissors*
- *Wooden skewer or cocktail stick*
- *Baking tin 230mm (9in) diameter*
- *Sesame seeds and poppy seeds*
- *Giant paper-clip*
- *Paint*
- *Varnish*

1 Make a plaited garland as for the Plaited Garland with fruit and flowers project. Working with the join at the top and following the instructions in Basic Techniques, make three French sticks and lay them over the join. Add two cottage loaves, two coburgs and two knots, evenly spaced around the ring.

2 Add groups of three sesame seed buns between each loaf, alternating between the inside edge and outside edge of the ring. Add pairs of wheat ears opposite the sesame buns, again alternating between the inside and outside edges of the garland.

3 Finally, add a few small leaves dotted between the breads, and fill in any spaces with a small ball of dough with a clove pushed into the centre.

4 Push a giant paper-clip well into the dough, as this is a particularly heavy piece and requires a strong hanger. Bake, paint the leaves if desired and varnish as instructed in Basic Techniques.

HEART-SHAPED GARLAND

These heart-shaped versions of the basic fruit and rose garlands make a superb gift for a wedding or anniversary as well as Valentine's Day. To personalise the gift, you could add a banner of dough across the garland with a date or initials.

To make either heart you will need:

- *2 cups flour made into dough (see page 11)*
- *Wooden skewer or cocktail stick*
- *Cloves*
- *Giant paper-clip*
- *Paint*
- *Varnish*

1 Use the trace-off template as a guide (see page 119). If you prefer, trace the template on to greaseproof paper, place this on your baking sheet and work directly on to it. Roll out two sausages of dough each approximately 19mm (¾in) diameter and 254mm (10in) long. Place these around the edges of the template to form the two sides of the heart. Flatten out slightly and then place fourteen moulded leaves along the garland.

2 For the fruit garland, add two apples, two pears and two oranges in the centre of the heart as shown. Place a leaf and five strawberries with a flower to the left, and a leaf with a bunch of grapes to the right. Fill in any spaces with plums and currants.

3 For the rose heart, place a cluster of full-blown roses in the centre of the heart and add some pointed leaves around the edges and in between some of the roses. Fill in any spaces with rosebuds made as instructed in Basic Techniques. Add a giant paper-clip for a hanger in the centre of the garland.

4 If you wish to add a banner, roll out a strip of dough 6mm (¼in) thick and cut to a ribbon 25mm (1in) wide. The centre of the banner will need supporting to prevent it from drooping in the middle, crunch up a piece of tin foil to form a bridge across the heart. To write on the banner, use the pointed end of a skewer or cocktail stick, and prick the letters into the dough rather than dragging the stick across it.

5 Bake, paint as desired and varnish as instructed in Basic Techniques.

*A*ll sorts of nuts, seed pods and pine cones gathered in the autumn make lovely decorations for a piece of dough. They are simply brushed with water and pressed into the raw dough. Once baked, they are firmly anchored in place ready for varnishing. More delicate items, such as dried flowers or ears of wheat, may be attached after varnishing with an all-purpose adhesive.

To make an autumn garland you will need:
- *2 cups flour made into dough (see page 11)*
- *Baking tin approximately 230mm (9in) diameter*
- *Selection of nuts, cones, seeds, grasses, dried or silk flowers etc.*
- *Large paper-clip*
- *Varnish*

1 The base of the garland can be any type of ring you like. Generally speaking, a thicker garland, such as a plaited ring or one with leaves, is preferable, as it gives you a good base to press your decoration into.

2 Make the garland of your choice following the instructions in Basic Techniques, and then simply add your decoration, leaving as much or as little of the dough showing as you desire.

3 A simpler flat cut-out ring can look attractive with a few ears of wheat glued on to it, and perhaps a little mouse crawling up the side.

4 Push a large paper-clip into the top for a hanger. Bake and varnish as instructed in Basic Techniques. Glue any dried or delicate material into place after the varnish is dry.

FRUIT BASKETS

Choose any fruit to make these simple baskets and match them to your decor. The baskets are shown in a choice of sizes, and the templates for cutting them can be found on pages 120–22.

To make one large and one small basket you will need:

- *2 cups flour made into dough (see page 11)*
- *Wooden skewer or cocktail stick*
- *Cloves*
- *Large paper-clips*
- *Paint*
- *Varnish*

1 Following the instructions given in Basic Techniques and using the trace-off template (see pages 120–22), make a basket. Using a wooden skewer or cocktail stick, mark the basket weave. For the large basket make twelve leaves and, using a little water, attach them to the basket as shown in the diagram.

3 Push a large paper-clip between the two central top leaves for hanging – this takes the pressure off the handle when you hang your dough on the wall. This is not necessary with the small basket as it is much lighter and the handle is thin enough to hang on a picture pin. Bake, paint as desired and varnish as instructed in Basic Techniques.

2 Make the fruit of your choice as instructed in Basic Techniques, and place on the basket in the centre of the leaves as shown. Add a few extra cut leaves tucked in between the pieces of fruit.

The small basket is made in exactly the same way, but with everything scaled down and using seven leaves instead of twelve around the edge of the fruit.

MIXED FRUIT BASKET

This luxurious and colourful basket of fruit is a development of the Fruit Basket project and is made using exactly the same method.

To make the mixed fruit basket you will need:

- *2 cups flour made into dough (see page 11)*
- *Wooden skewer or cocktail stick*
- *Cloves*
- *Large paper-clip*
- *Paint*
- *Varnish*

1 Using the trace-off template (see page 121), make your basket as instructed in Basic Techniques. Make about twenty leaves, moisten with a little water and position them around the basket.

2 Make two each of the following fruits – apples, oranges, pears and lemons. Arrange on the basket as shown in the diagram.

3 Add a cluster of strawberries and a strawberry flower on one side of the basket, and a bunch of grapes spilling out of the basket on the other side. Fill in the spaces between the fruits with currants, plums and a few small leaves.

4 Push a large paper-clip into the centre of the fruit at the top to take the pressure off the handle when hanging on the wall. Bake, paint and varnish as instructed in Basic Techniques.

SUMMER FRUIT BASKETS

These lovely summery projects are very similar to the simple fruit baskets, but the extra detail makes them a little more interesting, and the bright colour makes a particularly eye-catching piece.

To make one of these baskets you will need:

- 2 cups flour made into dough (see page 11)
- Fork
- Cloves (for the strawberries)
- Florist's wire (for the cherries)
- Large paper-clip
- Paint
- Varnish

1 Using the trace-off template (see page 120) make a basket as instructed in Basic Techniques. Mark the weave using the prongs of a fork. Make twelve leaves and position around the basket as shown in the diagram.

3 Add a few small leaves and small flowers dotted amongst the fruit.

2 Make and add your fruit, heaping it on to the basket to give a luxurious effect. For the strawberry basket, make some of the strawberries with the star-shaped stalk on top and the rest with a headless clove pushed into them as shown in Basic Techniques. For the cherry basket, push holes into the cherries with a cocktail stick and add pieces of florist's wire cut to approximately 50mm (2in) long. Bend a slight curve to a few of them to form a stalk.

4 Push a large paper-clip into the centre of the fruit at the top for hanging. Bake, paint and varnish as instructed in Basic Techniques.

ROSE BASKET

This project is a more advanced version of the Strawberry and Cherry Baskets. If you find the basket weaving too complicated you could use one of the simpler styles, such as that used for the fruit baskets. The roses can be painted in a variety of colours or in several different shades of the same basic colour.

To make the rose basket you will need:
- *2 cups flour made into dough (see page 11)*
- *Sharp knife*
- *Wooden skewer or cocktail stick*
- *Large paper-clip*
- *Paint*
- *Varnish*

1 Using the trace-off template (see page 122), make a woven basket as instructed in Basic Techniques, covering the bottom half of the template base below the dotted line with the woven strips. Place moulded rose leaves all round the top edge of the base and across the top of the basket as shown in the diagram, using a little water to attach them.

2 Fill in the top of the base with full-blown roses, made according to the instructions in Basic Techniques and taking care not to pack them too tightly so they get squashed.

3 Add several small leaves between the roses and fill in any remaining spaces with buds.

4 Push a large paper-clip for hanging into the centre of the model at the top ensuring that it is secure. Bake, paint and varnish as instructed in Basic Techniques.

BREAD BASKET

Although containing little colour, this piece looks extremely effective and makes a stunning kitchen decoration. The basket also matches the Bread and Wheat Ring in Chapter 3 and, together, they make an attractive pair.

To make the bread basket you will need:

- *2 cups flour made into dough (see page 11)*
- *Poppy and sesame seeds*
- *Fork and small scissors*
- *Wooden skewer or cocktail stick*
- *Cloves*
- *Paper-clip*
- *Paint and varnish*

1 Roll out half the dough to 6mm (¼in) thick and following the trace-off template (see page 121), make a basket, using the prongs of a fork to create the weave as shown in Basic Techniques.

three French sticks
two cottage loaves
two coburgs
two knots
three sesame seed buns
three poppy seed buns

2 Assemble the bows by placing two thick triangles of dough at each end of the handle and adding the ribbons cut from a flattened piece of dough as shown in the diagram.

3 Make the bread to fill the basket. You will require the following, made according to the instructions in Basic Techniques:

4 Having made the bread, assemble it in the basket as shown in the photograph. Fill in the spaces between the loaves with ears of wheat, small leaves and small balls of dough with a clove pressed into the centre.

5 Add a large paper-clip in the centre of the basket for hanging. Bake, then paint the bows in the colour of your choice, the leaves green and then varnish as instructed in Basic Techniques.

AUTUMN BASKET

As with the Autumn Garland, this is a simple project using salt dough as a basis for a collection of nuts, spices, pine cones etc.

To make the autumn basket you will need:

- *1 cup flour made into dough (see page 11)*
- *Wooden skewer or cocktail stick*
- *Knife*
- *Selection of nuts, cones, grasses, dried flowers etc*
- *Large paper-clip*
- *Varnish*

1 Using the trace-off template (see page 120), make a simple basket with leaves added to it, as instructed in the Fruit Baskets project (see page 60).

3 Push a paper-clip hanger into the top of your basket. Bake, then varnish as instructed in Basic Techniques.

2 Arrange your collection of nuts, seed pods, cones etc on the basket, making sure that you have moistened them with water. Once baked they will be firmly attached to the dough. Spices, such as pieces of cinnamon stick and star anise, add variety and interest. Fill in any spaces with small leaves, and/or small balls of dough with a clove pushed into the centre.

An alternative to the method used above involves sticking dried flowers or grasses to a plain, baked basket using an all-purpose adhesive.

The vegetables in this favourite design look almost good enough to eat! This is not the simplest project and requires particular care in judging the centre of gravity so that the basket doesn't hang drunkenly on the wall!

To make the vegetable trug you will need:

- *2 cups flour made into dough (see page 11)*
- *Small cloves*
- *Garlic press*
- *Wooden skewer or cocktail stick*
- *Giant paper-clip*
- *Paint*
- *Varnish*

1 Using the trace-off template (see page 119), make the trug-shaped basket with the overlapped strips of dough as instructed in Basic Techniques. Mark the centre of the basket and immediately to the left of the centre place a rolled out piece of dough 76 × 25mm (3 × 1in), as shown in the diagram. This forms a base for the handle.

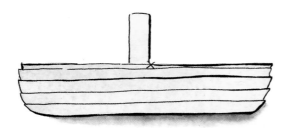

2 Roll a strip of dough 25mm (1in) wide by approximately 230mm (9in) long. Lay this on the baking tray adjacent to the handle base. Fold over and lay the remainder of the strip on top of the handle base, continuing across the centre of the basket, as shown in the diagram. Trim the end off, level with the base of the basket.

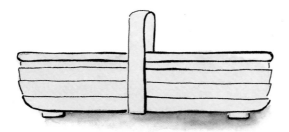

3 Make a selection of vegetables, (as shown in the photograph) according to the instructions in Basic Techniques, and lay them along the top edge of the trug, ensuring that they are dampened slightly and are touching the top of the basket. Begin at the centre, with the cabbage resting on the handle, then add the potatoes and leeks. Place the tomatoes between and slightly on top of the potatoes and leeks.

4 Next, beginning with the carrots, work outwards from the centre on the left-hand side of the basket, adding the cauliflower and green beans. Place a few mushrooms between and slightly overlapping the cauliflower and beans. You may, of course, substitute other vegetables of your choice.

5 Push a giant paper-clip into the top of the handle for hanging, ensuring that it is well embedded in the dough. Bake, paint and varnish as instructed in Basic Techniques.

CORNUCOPIA

This glorious horn of plenty with fruit spilling over the edge is assembled from relatively simple individual pieces. The overlapped style of basket produces a heavier base to counterbalance the mass of fruit at the top.

1 Roll out half the dough to approximately 6mm (¼in) thick and then, using the trace-off template (see page 122), cut out the basic horn shape and place on your baking sheet.

2 Re-roll the trimmings and cut into strips approximately 13mm (½in) wide at one end, and 19mm (¾in) wide at the other end. The longest strip needed is 203mm (8in). Using the template as a guide and starting at the dotted line, lay the strips overlapping each other down to the point of the horn, with the narrower ends along the curved inside edge of the horn. Once the bottom half of the base is covered, trim the strips off level with the base.

3 Lay leaves around the edge as shown.

4 Form the pineapple by flattening an oval ball of dough and marking diagonal lines in both directions with the back of a knife. Push a clove, without the seed heads into each square. The leaves are formed by flattening thin pointed strips.

To make the cornucopia you will need:

- *3 cups flour made into dough (see page 11)*
- *Cloves*
- *Knife*
- *Wooden skewer or cocktail stick*
- *Giant paper-clip*
- *Paint*
- *Varnish*

5 Place the apple, oranges and pears in position, (see Basic Techniques), then the five strawberries. Dot the seeds on to the strawberries with a skewer after positioning them. Add one or two small flowers to the group of strawberries.

6 Place grapes in the space between the pineapple and the other fruit. Making a pile of grapes and placing in position, will achieve a more natural effect than individual positioning.

7 Lastly, lay the ears of wheat alongside the fruit and fill in any spaces with plums or currants, bearing in mind the colours you will be painting them. Add a couple of twists of vine to the grapes and along the basket.

8 Push a giant paper-clip for hanging into the top of the pineapple. Bake, paint and varnish as instructed in Basic Techniques.

5
TREES AND PLANTS

MUSHROOMS

This simple project can be made by a complete beginner. The mushrooms may be left natural or painted and as many as you like may be added to the clusters to give a variety of shapes and sizes. Children can easily make a single mushroom or toadstool and like to paint them in bright colours.

To make the basic group of five mushrooms you will need:

- *1 cup flour made into dough (see page 11)*
- *Garlic press or potato ricer*
- *Knife*
- *Paper-clip*
- *Paint*
- *Varnish*

1 Roll out a long sausage of dough and cut into five pieces – one × 64mm (2½in) long, two × 76mm (3in) long, one × 102mm (4in) long and one × 127mm (5in) long. Arrange these together on your baking sheet as shown, laying the shortest piece centrally on top of the others.

2 Form the tops of the toadstools by taking a golf-ball-sized piece of dough, rolling it into a smooth ball and gently working a hollow centre with your thumb. Place one of these on the top ends of both the second and central stalk.

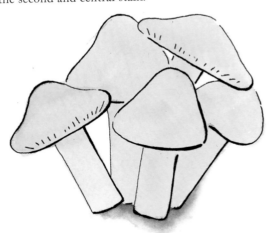

3 Form the flat mushroom tops by taking a slightly smaller ball of dough and working it into a flat head, slightly pointed on the top. Moisten the ends of the first and third stalks and attach the heads. Mark the gills on the underside of these flat mushrooms using a sharp knife.

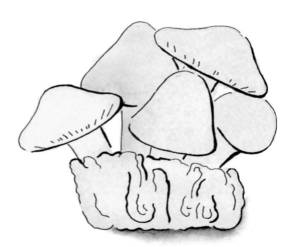

4 Lastly, take a ball of dough 25mm (1in) in diameter and press a hollow centre with your thumb to produce a button mushroom for the last stalk. Add extruded dough pressed through a garlic press or potato ricer at the base for grass, and a paper-clip at the top for hanging.

5 Bake, paint if desired and varnish as instructed in Basic Techniques.

TREES

The number of different designs for trees is almost endless. Simply follow the instructions in Basic Techniques and create your own combination of trunk, leaves and pot! The designs illustrated are an apple and bay tree.

To make one tree you will need:
- *2 cups flour made into dough (see page 11)*
- *Potato ricer or garlic press*
- *Paper-clip*
- *Paint*
- *Varnish*

APPLE TREE

1 Make a split trunk approximately 203mm (8in) long, as shown in Basic Techniques. Separate the branches out at the top and place a number of flattened balls of dough around the branches.

2 Cover each ball of dough with 'pinched' leaves and add small pea-sized apples dotted over the leaves.

3 Finish off the base of the tree with a mound of extruded dough grass.

4 Push a paper-clip hanger into the top of the tree. Bake, paint and varnish as instructed in Basic Techniques.

BAY TREE

1 The trunk here is simply a roll of dough 152mm (6in) long which can be twisted slightly to give a more natural appearance. Place a flattened ball of dough approximately 76mm (3in) in diameter at the top of the trunk and cut a dough flowerpot for the bottom. Make sure that the trunk extends beneath both the pot and the top of the tree.

2 Make many small, moulded leaves approximately 25mm (1in) in length, and place them all the way round the edge of the tree top as shown. Fill the rest of the tree top with leaves arranged like the petals of a flower.

3 Push a paper-clip hanger into the top of the tree to hang it on the wall. Bake, paint and varnish as instructed in Basic Techniques.

*T*his is really just a tree with a bird in it, but it does remind me of the Christmas carol! It can be any sort of tree; I have chosen a more delicate and intricate one, with individually moulded leaves.

For this project you will need:

- *2 cups flour made into dough (see page 11)*
- *Wooden skewer or cocktail stick*
- *Small blossom cutter (optional)*
- *Small scissors*
- *Large paper-clip*
- *Paint*
- *Varnish*

I Make the trunk of the tree and the crown following the instructions for the Apple Tree project. Add a dough flower pot and cover the crown with small moulded leaves as for the bay tree.

3 Finally, add the bird. He is made from a small piece of dough, pointed at each end for the beak and tail, and with his wings snipped with scissors as shown. Mark an eye with a skewer or cocktail stick.

2 Instead of apples, add small pears among the leaves. A few little bits of white blossom dotted between the fruit are very attractive and make the tree a little more interesting. If you do not have a small cutter, such as the type used by cake decorators, you can substitute tiny, moulded daisy-like flowers (see Basic Techniques).

4 Add a large paper-clip for hanging. Bake, paint as desired and varnish as instructed in Basic Techniques.

*T*his original project was inspired by the wonderful harvest-time decorations seen in bakers' shops. The wheatsheaf can be made in any size, from a dinky little 76mm (3in), to the largest your oven will take.

To make a large sheaf you will need:

- *2 cups flour made into dough (see page 11)*
- *Small sharp scissors*
- *Wooden skewer or cocktail stick*
- *Giant paper-clip*
- *Varnish*

1 Roll out half the dough to 6mm (¼in) thick, and, using the trace-off template (see page 120), cut out the basic keyhole shape required for the base of the sheaf. Dampen the bottom half of the base from the dotted line downwards, and then roll out long straws of dough and lay them side by side across the base as shown in the diagram. Build up two layers of straws in this way.

2 For ears of wheat, roll out small cigar shapes approximately 64mm (2½in) long and 19mm (¾in) wide, and place them in overlapping rows all round the curved top edge of the keyhole shape, as shown in the diagram, ensuring that the final row covers the top end of the straws.

3 When all the ears of wheat are in place, snip them all with small pointed scissors, as instructed in Basic Techniques.

4 Finally, add a small mouse (see page 26) to the corn stalks.

5 Push a giant paper-clip into the top of your wheatsheaf. Bake and varnish as instructed in Basic Techniques and when dry, tie the sheaf with a ribbon.

6
FRUIT AND
FLOWERS

FRUIT CLUSTERS

A bowl of dough fruits makes an attractive change from wooden or plastic ones. They can be made life-size or smaller, like the ones used in the projects. Make them according to the instructions in Basic Techniques. If making large individual fruits, bake them more slowly, as they will need a very long time to dry right through to the centre, having a tendency to split if cooked too quickly.

This project is an alternative to individual fruits, and has different fruits clustered together on a base of leaves to make an attractive wall-hanging.

To make a fruit cluster you will need:

- *1 cup of flour made into dough (see page 11)*
- *Cloves*
- *Wooden skewer or cocktail stick*
- *Large paper-clip*
- *Paint*
- *Varnish*

1 Make a base from a flattened ball of dough and attach leaves all round the edge as shown. Make sure you leave a suitable place at the top for pushing in the paper-clip.

2 Place an apple, orange and pear, with a group of five strawberries and three plums into the centre of the cluster. Add a strawberry flower and fill in the spaces with currants.

3 Push a large paper-clip into the top for hanging, then bake, paint and varnish as instructed in Basic Techniques.

POT OF PANSIES

*T*his unusual project, painted in really vibrant colours, makes a stunning decoration – wonderful for brightening up a dull window-sill.

To make this project you will need:

- *2 cups flour made into dough (see page 11)*
- *Wooden skewer or cocktail stick*
- *Knife*
- *Giant paper-clip*
- *Paint*
- *Varnish*

1 Roll out half the dough to 6mm (⅛in) thick, and using the trace-off template (see page 123), cut out the basic shape. Re-roll the trimmings and cut out a second 'pot' using the lower section of the trace-off template. Place this on top of the lower half of the basic shape so that the flowerpot part of this project is of double thickness. Lay a strip of dough 25mm (1in) wide across the top to form the lip of the pot.

3 Make ten pansies according to the instructions in Basic Techniques and arrange a row of four across the centre, and then three each above and below. Finally tuck a few extra leaves in between the flowers.

2 Make and place moulded leaves, with the edges drawn up to form jagged edges, all the way round the top half of the basic shape, with one or two overlapping on to the pot, as shown in the diagram.

4 Push a giant paper-clip for hanging into the top of the flowers. Bake slowly, as the smooth pot part of this decoration has a tendency to rise and bubble if cooked too quickly. Paint as desired and varnish as instructed in Basic Techniques.

VASE OF ROSES

*B*oth this and the Jug of Mixed Flowers (overleaf) are variations on the Pot of Pansies (previous project), using different flowers and containers.

For this project you will need:
- *2 cups flour made into dough (see page 11)*
- *Wooden skewer or cocktail stick*
- *Giant paper-clip*
- *Paint*
- *Varnish*

1 Roll out half the dough to 6mm ($\frac{1}{4}$in) thick, and using the trace-off template (see page 124), cut out the basic shape. Cut another rolled out piece of dough to the shape of the vase and, after dampening the base, lay this over the vase section so that it forms a double layer.

3 Fill in the flowered top with a mass of roses, mostly full-blown with a few buds tucked in the spaces. Tuck a few leaves in between the roses.

2 Make and lay leaves all around the flowered top with one or two overlapping on to the vase.

4 Add a giant paper-clip for hanging and bake slowly, as the smooth area of the vase has a tendency to rise and bubble if cooked too quickly. Paint as desired and varnish as instructed in Basic Techniques.

JUG OF MIXED FLOWERS

This colourful jug of flowers gives you a chance to use your own imagination. By combining several of the techniques already learnt in previous projects, you can produce a truly original piece of work.

To make a large jug of flowers you will need:

- *2 cups flour made into dough (see page 11)*
- *Wooden skewer or cocktail stick*
- *Knife*
- *Giant paper-clip*
- *Paint*
- *Varnish*

1 Roll out half your dough to 6mm ($\frac{1}{4}$in) thick, and using the trace-off template (see page 125), cut out the whole shape. Using the same technique as in the Pot of Pansies (page 90), cut another jug and lay it on top of the base. Roll out a long sausage of dough approximately 152mm (6in) long, and attach this with a little water to the side of the jug to form the handle as shown.

2 Making leaves of your choice, lay them all around the flowered top, with a few overlapping on to the jug. Add a profusion of different flowers of your choice to make a lovely summer bouquet. You could make the flowers as instructed in Basic Techniques, but if you feel like being a little more adventurous, design a few new ones of your own. You can also experiment with making some of them from a side view, or in different stages of opening.

3 Push a giant paper-clip into the top of your flowers, estimating the centre of gravity so the model hangs straight. Bake slowly to avoid the dough rising, paint in colours of your choice and varnish as instructed in Basic Techniques.

7
WALL
PLAQUES

WOODLAND SCENE

*A*mazingly, if you take a piece of wood, wet it, arrange some dough on top, and bake it in the oven, the dough sticks fast to the wood. There are many ideas which take advantage of this property of salt dough, such as using a wooden spoon as your base and adding face and hair to make a puppet. For this project, however, we use a pre-cut slice from a tree trunk, as readily available from florists' shops. Take care not to buy one that is already varnished.

To make the woodland scene you will need:
- *1 cup flour made into dough (see page 11)*
- *Wooden base*
- *Wooden skewer or cocktail stick*
- *Small scissors*
- *Black-headed map pin*
- *2 picture eyes*
- *Varnish*

1 Using your wooden base instead of a baking tray, first form a tree in the top half of the wood, following the instructions in Chapter 5 (see page 80).

2 At the base of the tree add some extruded dough grass, a hedgehog (see page 26) and a few leaves.

3 Bake and varnish as instructed in Basic Techniques. Once the varnish is dry, screw two picture eyes into the back of the wooden plaque and thread some string through them to hang your project on the wall.

This project can be varied in many ways; use your wooden base in the landscape (horizontal) rather than portrait (vertical) position, or paint all or part of the dough model. You can of course use a wooden base for other projects as well. They make particularly good name plates, although they are not suitable for outside use.

THATCHED COTTAGE

This is another project which lends itself to a little improvisation. You could work according to the basic directions, or have fun changing details to suit yourself. For example, why not change the position of windows and doors or paint the model in different colours? Or why not model your own house in dough?

To make a thatched cottage you will need:

- *2 cups flour made into dough (see page 11)*
- *Knife*
- *Potato ricer (preferably) or garlic press*
- *Wooden skewer or cocktail stick*
- *Large paper-clip*
- *Paint*
- *Varnish*

1 Using the trace-off template (see page 123), cut the shape for the cottage from dough rolled out to 6mm ($\frac{1}{4}$in) thick. Add a door frame made from thin strips of dough, and then mark the wooden planks of the door within the frame with a knife. Add window frames in the same way.

2 Construct the roof overhang over one of the windows from thinly rolled out dough, supported on a 'sausage' of dough placed just above the window frame. Cover the roof, apart from the chimney, in thatch made from extruded dough, adding a prettily shaped ridge at the top cut from thinly rolled out dough.

3 Place flowers round the door, and leaves and grass along the base of the house.

4 Push a large paper-clip into the top, calculating the centre of gravity. Bake, paint as desired and varnish as instructed in Basic Techniques.

*T*hese pretty wall-hangings can be made in a range of sizes, with different coloured ribbons and types of flowers.

To make a medium-sized hat you will need:

- *1 cup flour made into dough (see page 11)*
- *Saucer*
- *Fork*
- *Wooden skewer or cocktail stick*
- *Small paper-clip*
- *Paint*
- *Varnish*

1 Roll a ball of dough the size of a walnut and place it on your baking tray. Roll out the remainder of your dough 6mm (¼in) thick, and using a saucer as your guide, cut a circle. Mark the edge of the circle all the way round with the prongs of a fork to give a fancy edge. Lay the circle centrally over the ball of dough on your baking sheet.

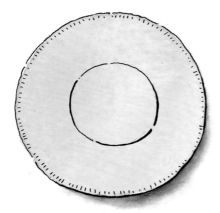

2 For the ribbon, roll out a long, thin strip of dough approximately 13mm (½in) wide and 305mm (12in) long. Lay this around the crown of the hat and form a bow as shown in the diagram.

3 Make and place three small leaves and a flower over the centre of the bow.

4 Make three small sausage-shaped pieces of dough and tuck them under the brim of the hat – one at the top and the other two at each side, to give a wavy effect in the brim.

5 Push a small paper-clip into the support at the top of the brim. Bake, paint the ribbon and flowers and varnish as instructed in Basic Techniques.

*T*his set of small wall plaques depicts the four seasons, but the idea can be adapted to any images. For example, a set of four plaques could show different flowers or animals.

To make four small plaques you will need:

- *3 cups flour made into dough (see page 11)*
- *Saucer*
- *Wooden skewer or cocktail stick*
- *Potato ricer or garlic press*
- *Small scissors*
- *Large paper-clips*
- *Paint*
- *Varnish*

Spring

Summer

1 Roll out your dough to approximately 13mm ($\frac{1}{2}$in) thick, and, using a saucer as a template, cut four circles. The spring scene has a rabbit amongst some daffodils. Following the instructions in Basic Techniques for the daffodils, and Chapter 2 for the rabbit (see pages 36–7), build up your picture. Add some extra leaves around the flowers and some extruded dough grass at the bottom.

2 The summer scene is a beautiful bouquet of roses. Following the instructions in Basic Techniques, place a group of full-blown roses centrally on the plaque. Fill in between them with buds and leaves, and tuck leaves underneath the roses all around the outside.

Autumn

Winter

3 The autumn plaque is constructed in the same way, but with corn and mice in place of the daffodils and rabbit. Following the instructions in Chapter 2, make two small mice (see page 26) and place them at the base of your plaque. Roll out some long thin stalks for the corn and place them running up the right-hand side of your plaque. Make a few cigar-shaped ears of wheat and, having snipped them with sharp scissors, place them at the top of the corn stalks. Add a little extruded dough grass around the base.

4 The winter scene shows a traditional snowman. He is easily constructed from two balls of dough for the head and body with the usual additions of hat, scarf, buttons and carrot nose. Mark the eyes with a wooden skewer or cocktail stick. A piece of flattened dough at the base makes the snow-covered ground, and small dots of dough the falling snow.

5 Push a paper-clip hanger into the top of each plaque. Bake, paint as desired and varnish.

HARVEST PLAQUE

This piece was inspired by a sketch in our local church magazine at harvest time. The abundance of fruit, vegetables and bread give this project a real 'fruits of the earth' appeal.

To make the harvest plaque you will need:

- *2 cups flour made into dough (see page 11)*
- *Cloves*
- *Small scissors*
- *Wooden skewer or cocktail stick*
- *Giant paper-clip*
- *Paint*
- *Varnish*

1 Roll out half your dough to approximately 13mm (½in) thick and, using the trace-off template (see page 126), cut out an oval shape. Make and place a small basket slightly left of centre of the plaque and fill with an assortment of small vegetables of your choice, made according to the instructions in Basic Techniques.

3 Arrange a bunch of wheat, made in the same way as in the Wheatsheaf project, with the stalks running up the right-hand side of the plaque and the ears curling around the top.

2 Around the base of the basket arrange a group of bread rolls and individual fruits, made according to the instructions in Basic Techniques.

4 Add a giant paper-clip pushed into the top. Bake, paint and varnish as instructed in Basic Techniques.

*T*his and the following four plaques are constructed as a variation on the same theme, thus providing a matching set should you want to make a collection.

This charming cockerel is not as difficult to construct as it looks, and once you have mastered the art of producing the basic plaque, you can put any animal you fancy into the field!

A word of warning – large, heavy pieces of dough such as this are more susceptible than smaller pieces to stresses in the dough and are more inclined to crack (see Troubleshooting). This can be heartbreaking when you have spent a lot of time constructing your piece, so it is worth taking every precaution to stop this happening. A laminated dough (instructions follow) should help to prevent cracks, and also cooking your dough at a lower temperature

(maximum 110°C/225°F/Gas Mark $\frac{1}{4}$) for a longer period. This may take up to forty-eight hours, after which you should cool it down slowly by gradually reducing the oven temperature. Once you have switched the oven off, leave the plaque in the oven to cool off completely.

For the cockerel plaque you will need:
- *3 cups flour made into dough (see page 11)*
- *Piece of nylon tulle netting 254mm (10in) square*
- *Knife*
- *Wooden skewer or cocktail stick*
- *Clove*
- *Potato ricer or garlic press*
- *Giant paper-clip*
- *Paint*
- *Varnish*

1 To laminate dough, first cut the net to the shape of the plaque, using the trace-off template (see page 126). Roll out half the dough into a long oval shape approximately 508mm (20in) × 254mm (10in) × 6mm ($\frac{1}{4}$in) thick. Brush the dough with water and lay the net on the upper half as shown. Fold up the lower half of the dough so it lays on top of the netting. Re-roll the two layers together to make sure that the netting is well embedded into the dough. Your plaque should be about 10mm ($\frac{3}{8}$in) thick. This laminating process helps to prevent cracking once the dough is cooked.

2 Using the template again, cut your laminated plaque to the required shape and size with a sharp knife, trying to keep the template centrally over the netting. Any bits of netting left protruding from the edges can be cut off with scissors after cooking. Transfer on to a baking sheet and moisten the surface with a little water. Add the fence, formed from flattened snakes of dough, across the centre of the plaque in a slightly curved line. Place four fence posts made in the same way on the top.

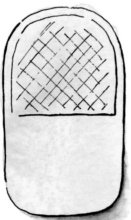

3 Add the tree next. Form the trunk as shown in Basic Techniques and place it between the two central fence posts. Add pinched dough leaves and small balls of dough for apples. It is a good idea to add a paper-clip at centre top at this stage, as if it pushes the dough out of shape, a few more leaves on the tree will disguise this.

You now have your basic plaque, ready to add the animals of your choice – in this case a cockerel.

4 To make the cockerel, first form the head and body all in one piece from a smoothly rolled piece of dough the size of an orange. Form the dough into an elongated shape and gently narrow one end for the head, then flatten and bend into shape as shown. Lay on to the plaque over the base of the tree trunk.

5 Add an elongated wing made from a flattened cone of dough marked with a paper-clip. Form a small beak between thumb and forefinger and attach to the head with a little water. The cockscomb is cut with scissors from a flattened ball of dough and then attached to the top of the head.

Small, flattened teardrop-shaped pieces of dough are added just below the centre of this for the eye, and below the beak for the crop.

6 The magnificent tail is made by hand rolling lots of dough 'worms' of different lengths, and piling them on top of each other. The legs are thinly rolled pieces of dough placed just under the body. Mark faint lines gently across the legs with a sharp knife. Claws are carefully moulded from tiny pieces of dough and added to the foot of the raised leg.

7 The piece is finished by adding grass along the bottom edge of the plaque, made from dough extruded through a garlic press or potato ricer. Add a few leaves and flowers.

8 Bake as instructed at the beginning of the project. The painting of the cockscomb in a vibrant red and the electric blue of the tail add to its attraction. Varnish as instructed in Basic Techniques.

DUCK WALL PLAQUE

This second piece in the set of plaques is constructed in the same way as the previous project but is simpler to make. Ducks are a favourite with many people and these three fit beautifully on to a wall plaque (see page 2).

For the duck plaque you will need:

- *3 cups flour made into dough (see page 11)*
- *Piece of nylon tulle netting 254mm (10in) square*
- *Knife*
- *Wooden skewer or cocktail stick*
- *Cloves*
- *Potato ricer or garlic press*
- *Giant paper-clip*
- *Paint*
- *Varnish*

1 Follow steps 1, 2 and 3, as for the Cockerel Plaque.

2 Add the first duck by placing a flattened piece of dough against the tree in the centre. Make the head and beak as instructed for the ducks in Chapter 2 (see page 30).

3 Add the other two ducks as shown in the diagram, constructing them as shown in Chapter 2 (see page 30). Place bows at their necks and tuck feet under their bodies.

4 Add extruded dough grass at the bottom of the plaque and a few leaves and flowers to fill in the spaces at the side.

5 Bake as instructed for the Cockerel Plaque, paint as desired and varnish as instructed in Basic Techniques.

PIG WALL PLAQUE

*G*loucester Old Spot pigs snuffling around in an orchard make a charming, old-fashioned rural scene, with the style of the pigs adding a comic touch.

For the pig plaque you will need:

- *3 cups flour made into dough (see page 11)*
- *Piece of nylon tulle netting 254mm (10in) square*
- *Knife*
- *Wooden skewer or cocktail stick*
- *Potato ricer or garlic press*
- *Giant paper-clip*
- *Paint*
- *Varnish*

1 Follow steps 1, 2 and 3, as for the Cockerel Plaque.

2 Once you have the basic plaque consisting of field, fence and tree, simply fill the field with pigs! You can add a mother pig with piglets, and individual pigs shown from both front and side views as in the photograph. Instructions for pigs can be found in Chapter 2 (see page 32) – just make them a little smaller to be in scale with the field.

3 Dot a few leaves and daisies (see Basic Techniques) between the pigs in the field, and add extruded dough grass in small clumps around the flowers and along the bottom edge of the plaque.

4 Bake as instructed for the Cockerel Plaque, paint as desired and varnish as instructed in Basic Techniques.

SHEEP WALL PLAQUE

*T*his rather more complicated variation of the wall plaques was inspired by a beautiful terracotta wall-hanging in a friend's kitchen.

For the sheep plaque you will need:

- *3 cups flour made into dough (see page 11)*
- *Piece of nylon tulle netting 254mm (10in) square*
- *Knife*
- *Wooden skewer or cocktail stick*
- *Potato ricer or garlic press*
- *Giant paper-clip*
- *Paint*
- *Varnish*

1 Follow steps 1, 2 and 3, as for the Cockerel Plaque.

2 Once you have the fence and tree in place, add the shepherd. Working from the top down, make the crown of the hat first and then attach a brim to it. Place a small ball of dough below the hat for the head, and using the wooden skewer mark in the hair and features. Don't worry too much about accuracy – just get the general impression of a face.

3 Tuck one small sausage-shaped arm underneath a triangular-shaped smock, and place the other arm on top, making creases in the smock fabric with the skewer. Add a piece of broken wooden skewer for his crook, and then place small balls of dough for hands. Lastly, add a scarf around his neck.

4 Make several fat sausage shapes for the sheep's bodies and arrange them around the shepherd. Next, add heads to all the sheep, facing them in different directions, with ears on each head.

5 Mark the sheep's wool with the blunt end of a wooden skewer, and mark eyes and noses with the pointed end. Place extruded dough grass along the base of the plaque.

6 Bake according to the directions for the Cockerel Plaque. Paint as desired and varnish as instructed in Basic Techniques.

COW AND GOOSE WALL PLAQUE

*I*nspiration for this scene came from an illustration of a farm in the Yorkshire Dales. One can almost imagine the cow beneath the trees to be part of the farmer's family!

For this project you will need:

- *3 cups flour made into dough (see page 11)*
- *Piece of nylon tulle netting 254mm (10in) square*
- *Knife*
- *Wooden skewer or cocktail stick*
- *Potato ricer or garlic press*
- *Giant paper-clip*
- *Paint*
- *Varnish*

1 Follow steps 1, 2 and 3, as for the Cockerel Plaque.

2 Add a cow to your field, following the instructions in Chapter 2 (see page 40), but make your cow smaller so that it is in scale with its surroundings.

Shape for Geese

3 Make two geese by rolling out two pieces of dough to the shape shown in the diagram, bending the necks up. Add wings, beaks and feet as shown.

4 Dot a few leaves, daisies and tufts of grass around between the animals, and add extruded dough grass along the base of the plaque.

5 Bake according to the instructions for the Cockerel Plaque, paint as desired and varnish as instructed in Basic Techniques.

ACKNOWLEDGEMENTS

I would like to thank the following people who directly or indirectly have helped to put this book on the shelves.

My husband Ken for his help with the word processing, painting, varnishing and child-minding whilst I was working on the text. Friends, Elizabeth Cook, Linda Allen and Debbie Gooch, who helped to keep 'Dough Designs' in full production. My father for his book-keeping service, and my mother for her help with the children. Rosemary Stammers for inspiring me to try my hand at doughcraft in the first instance. Jane Greenoff for inspiring me to write.

FURTHER READING

Joner, Tone Bergli, *The Dough Book*, Broadcast Books Ltd, 1991

Jones, Joanna, *Decorative Dough*, Merehurst Ltd, 1993

Kiskalt, Isolde, *Dough Crafts*, Sterling/Lark, 1991

Porteous, Brenda, *Fun Dough*, David Porteous, 1992

INDEX